The FALLING AWAY

SPIRITUAL DEPARTURE OR PHYSICAL RAPTURE?

A second look at 2 Thessalonians 2:3

Dr. Andy Woods

DISPENSATIONAL
PUBLISHING HOUSE, INC.

All Scripture quotations, unless otherwise indicated,
are taken from the New American Standard Bible®,
Copyright © 1960, 1962, 1963, 1968, 1971, 1972, 1973, 1975, 1977, 1995
by The Lockman Foundation
Used by permission. (www.Lockman.org)

Printed in the U.S.A.
First Edition, Second Printing, 2018
ISBN: 978-1-945774-20-1

DispensationalPublishing House, Inc.
PO Box 3181, Taos, NM 87571

www.dispensationalpublishing.com

Orders by U.S. trade bookstores and wholesalers. Please contact the publisher:
Tel: (844) 321-4202

2 3 4 5 6 7 8 9 10 1

*This pamphlet is affectionately dedicated to
Dr. J. Dwight Pentecost (April 24, 1915 – April 28, 2014),
a long time professor of Bible Exposition at
Dallas Theological Seminary. I was privileged to have
him for four academic courses. He has exerted more
influence over the way I think about the Bible as a
whole than any other human teacher. It was from
him that I first learned of the physical departure
interpretation of Second Thessalonians 2:3a.*

Table of Contents

The Background

Perhaps one of the most enigmatic Bible verses in all the Scripture is found in Second Thessalonians 2:3, which says, "Let no one deceive you by any means; for that Day will not come unless the falling away comes first, and the man of sin is revealed, the son of perdition" (NKJV). The Apostle Paul had on his second missionary journey planted the church in Thessalonica. Within less than a year, Paul was forced out of Thessalonica by the unbelieving Jews that were persecuting him. Consequently, he was driven ultimately into Berea, then Athens, and finally Corinth. When Paul wrote the two Thessalonian epistles he was writing to the infant church that he had just planted about six months to a year earlier. Thus, his audience consisted primarily of new Christians, or what some might call today "baby Christians."

These folks were confused, to say the least. Why were they confused? The immediately preceding verse (2 Thess. 2:2), says, "not to be soon shaken in mind or troubled, either by spirit or by word or by letter, as if from us, as though the day of Christ had come." Apparently, during Paul's absence from Thessalonica a forged letter had begun to circulate in their midst, allegedly having come from Paul, telling the new Thessalonian believers that they were in the Tribulation period. When Paul was with them, about six months to a year later, he had taught them that they would be raptured to heaven prior to the Tribulation period (1 Thess. 1:10; 4:13-18). Now, because of this forged letter that had come into their midst, the Thessalonian Christians, thought that they were in the actual Tribulation period. This mindset was compounded by the fact that the unbelieving Jews that had persecuted Paul were now turning on Paul's flock in his absence. Keep in mind that most of the New Testament had not even been written yet. Beyond that, the apostle that led them to Christ was now absent. Because they were new Christians, with very little spiritual knowledge, they were shaken and confused because of the apparent inconsistency between Paul's initial teaching and his alleged letter to them.

Consequently, Paul responds in Second Thessalonians 2:3-12 by laying out five reasons why the Day of the Lord has not yet started. He explains that the Day of the Lord has not started yet because there is no apostasy (2:3a), advent of the lawless one or Antichrist (2:3a-4), removal of the restrainer (2:5-7), destruction of the lawless one (2:8-9), and destruction of the lawless one's followers (2:10-12).

Day of the Lord has not started yet because:
There is no apostasy (2:3a)
Advent of the lawless one or Antichrist (2:3a-4)
Removal of the restrainer (2:5-7)
Destruction of the lawless one (2:8-9)
Destruction of the lawless one's followers (2:10-12).

What we are focused on here is the first item that Paul mentions as to why his audience was not yet in the Day of the Lord, or the Tribulation period. Paul is clear that "first" must come the "apostasy" or the "falling away" (2:3a). The English expression "apostasy" or "falling away" comes from the Greek noun *apostasia*. There are two major views on what is meant through the noun *apostasia*. The majority view is that it is speaking of a spiritual departure, such as the unbelieving world embracing the Antichrist. Most Christians today believe that this is what is meant and that is the sign that Paul gives here. However, there is an entirely different view on this topic. According to the second view, the *apostasia* is not a spiritual departure but rather represents a physical or spatial departure. If this latter view is accurate, Paul's simple point to the Thessalonian believers is that they could not possibly be in the Tribulation period because their physical departure, or the pretribulation rapture that he had already taught you about, has not yet transpired.

What difference does it really make if Second Thessalonians 2:3a is speaking of a spiritual departure or a physical departure? The reason it matters is because there has been for over at least the last century a vigorous debate amongst those who believe in a future Tribulation period and subsequent kingdom, concerning the question, "When the rapture will take place relative to the coming Tribulation period?" *Pretribulationalists* believe that the rapture takes place before the Tribulation period begins. *Mid-tribulationalists* believe that the rapture is going to take place in the middle of the tribulation period. *Post-tribulationalists* believe that the rapture will take place at the end of the tribulation period. *Prewrath* rapturists contend that the rapture will take place at some point in the second half of the Tribulation period. If verse 3a, is talking about a physical departure and not a spiritual departure, then the debate concerning when the rapture will transpire is all but over. Paul says, "...that Day will not come unless the falling away comes first" (2 Thess. 2:3a). The word translated "first" is the Greek adjective *prōton*, which means "first of all." If a physical departure must first transpire before the Day of the Lord can even begin, then it becomes a decisive victory for *pretribulationalism*. Thus, how one interprets Second Thessalonians 2:3a is of grave consequence to the longstanding debate concerning the timing of the rapture.

I believe that what is being spoken of here is not a spiritual departure but rather a physical departure, which would be a great source of evidence favoring the pretribulational view. What I would like to present are ten reasons why I believe that the physical or spatial understanding of apostasia in Second Thessalonians 2:3a is the correct interpretation, and why the spiritual departure view is an inadequate interpretation.[1]

---

1 This article was originally published in *The Prophecy Watcher Magazine*. See Andy Woods, "2 Thessalonians 2:3a: Apostasy of Rapture?," *The Prophecy WatcherMay 2017*, 14-17, 34-35.

> *If verse 3a, is talking about a physical depar-*
> *ture and not a spiritual departure, then the*
> *debate concerning when the rapture will*
> *transpire is all but over.*

10

reasons the falling away refers to the Rapture

There Have Always Been Doctrinal Departures

S piritual departures are not abnormal. In fact, spiritual departures regularly transpire in Scripture going all the way back to the Fall of man as recorded in Genesis 3. Paul himself was the victim of wide-scale spiritual defection. Even though "all who lived in Asia heard the word of the Lord" (Acts 19:10) through Paul's prolific ministry in Ephesus on his third missionary journey, a short time later in his final letter written just prior to his death Paul reported that "all who are in Asia turned away from me" (2 Tim. 1:15). The Apostle Paul in his day also predicted a spiritual departure after the passing away of the apostolic generation. In Acts 20:28-31, he warned:

> [28] Be on guard for yourselves and for all the flock, among which the Holy Spirit has made you overseers, to shepherd the church of God which He purchased with His own blood. [29] I know that after my departure savage wolves will come in among you, not sparing the flock; [30] and from among your own selves men will arise, speaking perverse things, to draw away the disciples after them. [31] Therefore be on the alert, remembering that night and day for a period of three years I did not cease to admonish each one with tears.

Here, Paul predicted that after the apostolic generation left the scene there would be a wide-scale spiritual departure in the church. As one studies the last two thousand years of church history we can see how Paul's prophecy came to pass. There are perpetual spiritual departures.

For example, note the rules of Harvard University, which was founded in 1636:

> Let every student be plainly instructed, and earnestly pressed to consider that the main end of his life and studies is, to know God and Jesus Christ, which is eternal life, John 17:3, and therefore to lay Christ in

the bottom as the only foundation of all sound knowledge and learning. And seeing the Lord only giveth wisdom, let everyone seriously set himself to prayer in secret to seek it of Him, Proverbs 2 and 3. Everyone shall so exercise himself in reading the Scriptures twice a day, that he shall be ready to give such an account of his proficiency therein.[2]

I would say that Harvard University has spiritually departed from its founding standard, wouldn't you? My point here is that if spiritual departures are normative throughout history, how could yet another a spiritual departure function as a definitive sign of the beginning of the Tribulation period? Thus, Paul must be using the noun *apostasia* to communicate something more than a mere spiritual departure in Second Thessalonians 2:3a.

---

2   Cited in David Barton, *Original Intent: The Courts, the Constitution, & Religion*, 3d ed. (Aledo, TX: Wall Builder Press, 2000), 81.

Second Thessalonians Was an Early Letter

Both 1-2 Thessalonians were among the earliest letters that Paul wrote. Here is a brief chronology of Paul's letters. The first letter he wrote was the Book of Galatians, about A.D. 49. The next two letters he wrote around the same period and in very close proximity to one another are 1-2 Thessalonians around A.D. 51. Then later came the two Corinthian letters and Romans (A.D. 56-57). These letters were then followed by his "prison letters" (Ephesians, Colossians, Philemon, Philippians) written from A.D. 60-62. Finally, late in his ministry, Paul wrote letters to pastors, such as First Timothy and Titus (A.D. 62) and Second Timothy (A.D. 67). Thus, First and Second Thessalonians were probably written during the same year, with perhaps six months to a year at most between these two letters. Moreover, there is a very small amount of time between Paul's planting of the church in Thessalonica, which occurred during his second missionary journey, and when he wrote First and Second Thessalonians.

Brief chronology of Paul's letters	
Dates are approximate and A.D.	
49	Galatians
51	1-2 Thessalonians
56–57	1-2 Corinthians and Romans
60–62	Ephesians, Colossians, Philemon, Philippians
62	1 Timothy and Titus
67	2 Timothy

Why is this chronology relevant? Although Paul does deal with an immediate apostasy among his flock early on (Gal. 1:6-9), he does not start predicting and warning about a spiritual end time apostasy until much later in his ministry. End-time apostasy is not a topic on his mind early on. In fact, to my knowledge, the very first prediction that Paul gives concerning a coming spiritual departure is from the verses noted earlier at the end of his third missionary journey when he was speaking to the elders at Ephesus at Miletus (Acts 20:28-31). It is then in the Timothy letters, that Paul really starts predicting an end-time spiritual departure. While Paul does it some in First Timothy (1 Tim. 4:1ff), it becomes a massive subject in Second Timothy (2 Tim. 3:14–4:8). Although the Apostle Peter picks up this same theme in Second Peter, keep in mind that this book was also not written until very late, around A.D. 64. Then, the Lord's half-brother, Jude, writes a one chapter book, focusing intensely on the theme of an end-time spiritual apostasy in the book of Jude (A.D. 68-70).

So, what is my point? My point is that the concept of an end-time spiritual departure is not something that Paul is focused on early in his ministry. Although it becomes a big topic later, it is not a dominant subject when the church first started. As already noted First and Second Thessalonians were written very early on in Paul's ministry. Thus, it would be somewhat of an oddity for Paul to focus upon the subject of an end time spiritual departure in the very early Thessalonian epistles when this subject is not something that Paul emphasizes until much later in his life and ministry. In fact, as you study the Thessalonian books, outside of this single disputed verse (2 Thess. 2:3a), we do not find Paul using the word "apostasy" or even the concept.

3

The Definite Article Before the Noun

Apostasia

There is a definite article in front of the noun "apostasy." Second Thessalonians 2:3 says, "Let no one deceive you by any means; for *that Day will not come* unless the falling away comes first, and the man of sin is revealed, the son of perdition" (NKJV). Notice the definite article translated "the" in front of both "falling away" and "man of sin." By providing these two definite articles essentially Paul is indicating that the apostasy will be something that has specific, time bound-qualities just like the man of sin's coming has such qualities. In other words, just like the advent of the man of sin will be specific and an instantaneous event in future history, the coming *apostasia*, or departure, will similarly be specific and time bound.

The advent of the coming lawless one or Antichrist will take place at a specified point in time and instantaneously concurrently with the opening of the first seal judgment (Rev. 6:1-2). The definite article also before the apostasia indicates that in the same way the apostasia will also take place instantaneously. Such an instantaneous manifestation does not fit well with the notion of a spiritual departure, which typically transpires gradually over an elongated process. Spiritual departures are not instantaneous events. After all, it took the church at Ephesus three decades to spiritually depart from Christ by leaving its first love (Rev. 2:4-5). However, unlike gradual, spiritual departures, the rapture of the church will be an instantaneous event that will take place "in a moment, in the twinkling of an eye" (1 Cor. 15:51). Thus, the use of the two definite articles indicates that the apostasia will take place just as instantly as the coming forth of the lawless one. This understanding better harmonizes with interpreting "the apostasia" as the instantaneous removal of the church through the rapture rather than a gradual doctrinal erosion.

4

The Noun *Apostasia* Can Refer to a Physical Departure

The noun, *apostasia*, can refer to a physical departure. Those arguing for a doctrinal departure interpretation of Second Thessalonians 2:3a typically contend that the only other time that noun *apostasia* is used in the entire Greek New Testament is in Acts 21:21. This verse says "and they have been told about you, that you are teaching all the Jews who are among the Gentiles to forsake the law Moses." The noun translated "forsake" here is also the Greek noun *apostasia*. In other words, Paul was accused in Acts 21:21, in a totally different context, of leading a spiritual apostasy or departure away from the Law of Moses. Spiritual departure advocates of Second Thessalonians 2:3a contend that since the noun *apostasia* clearly means a spiritual departure in Acts 21:21, which is the only other time the noun is ever used in the Greek New Testament, then that is what the noun also must mean in Second Thessalonians 2:3a.

However, such methodology represents a shallow way of determining a word's meaning. Words mean things based upon their own unique context. When you travel to a removed, remote context in an entirely different book of the Bible that is the product of an entirely different human author to establish the meaning of a word, you are employing an inadequate method of interpretation since that remote context (Acts 21:21) most likely gives the same word *apostasia* an entirely different meaning than the one found in Second Thessalonians 2:3a. Although the Greek noun *apostasia* can refer to a doctrinal departure in Acts 21:21, this noun is not a technical word meaning a word that always means the same thing everywhere it is used.

The Greek noun *apostasia* is a compound word, which means that it is a word that is created by combining two previously existing words. The first word is the Greek preposition *apo*, which means "away from." The second word is the Greek verb *histēmi*, which means, "to stand." Thus, *apostasia* simply means to "to stand away from" or "to depart." The question then becomes depart from what? Only be examining how this word is used in its immediate context will determine what the departure is from, whether it be a spiritual or physical departure. Thus, *apostasia* does not inherently mean doctrinal departure, although it can mean that if the context calls for it. Furthermore, *apostasia* does not inherently mean physical departure, although (as I argue later) it can also mean that if the context demands it. Context them becomes the critical factor in determining what the *apostasia* or departure is from.

In actuality, the Greek noun *apostasia*, can in some contexts refer to a physical departure. We know this to be the case since Liddell and Scott, a well-known Greek lexicon, uses the following terms to define *apostasia*: "rebellion against God, apostasy, departure, disappearance, distance."[3] While the first two definitions favor a spiritual departure understanding, the latter three entries favor a physical or spatial departure view. Similarly, Lampe's *A Patristic Greek Lexicon* defines *apostasia* as "revolt, defection, apostasy (from paganism, Judaism, Christianity, orthodoxy), divorce, departure, standing aloof."[4] While the first three definitions favor a spiritual departure understanding, the latter three entries favor a physical or spatial departure view. H. Wayne House notes the chronological significance of these

---

3 Henry Liddell & Henry Scott, *A Greek English Lexicon* (Oxford: Oxford University Press, 1940), 218.

4 G. W. H. Lampe, *A Patristic Greek Lexicon* (Oxford: Clarnedon Press, 1961), 208.

two lexical sources and why they have a bearing on the meaning of the word *apostasia* during the New Testament period.

> The noun form allows for *apostasia* as a simple departure in the classical period, proved by examples from Liddell and Scott...If one says that this is not important because the meaning is only classical or ancient and thus lost its meaning by the time of the New Testament, then I may turn to the same root meaning of *apostasia* in the patristic era immediately following the New Testament period, as indicated in the definitions for the noun form in Lampe's *Patristic Greek Lexicon*. Although the noun used in the sense of spatial departure is not the normal meaning...during New Testament times, the word is found with this meaning in time periods before and after the New Testament era, and it is likely to have been understood this way at least sometimes.[5]

It is also worth considering that while *apostasia* is used in Second Thessalonians 2:3a, *apostasion* represents a nearly identical and highly related noun. Interestingly, the latter noun is used exclusively in the New Testament to describe the physical and spatial separation of a divorce (Matt. 5:31; 19:7; Mark 10:4). For example, Mark 10:4 says, "They said, 'Moses permitted *a man* TO WRITE A CERTIFICATE OF DIVORCE [*apostasion*] AND SEND *her* AWAY.'" Therefore, cumulatively considering all the lexical evidence, the noun, *apostasia*, can, in some contexts, refer to a physical or spatial removal, and therefore, as previously noted, cannot be a technical word.

---

5 H. Wayne House, "Apostasia in 2 Thessalonians 2:3: Apostasy of Rapture?," in *When the Trumpet Sounds: Today's Foremost Authorities Speak out on End-Time Controversies*, ed. Thomas Ice and Timothy Demy(Eugene, OR: Harvest House, 1995), 273.

5

The Verb *Aphistēmi* Can Refer to a Physical Departure

Words are ultimately derived from roots. From a common root one can develop both a noun form and a verbal form of a word. Sometimes in English we use the same word for both a noun and a verb. For example, if I said, "Jane went on a run," I would be using "run" as a noun. However, if I said "see Jan run," I would be using "run" as a verb. The verb form of the noun *apostasia* is the verb *aphistēmi*. Both the noun and verbal form emanate from the same root, (*hístēmi* – to cause to stand, to set or place).

As previously mentioned the noun *apostasia* is only mentioned twice in the Greek New Testament (Acts 21:21; 2 Thess. 2:3a). However, the verbal form *aphistēmi* is found 15 times in the New Testament. Interestingly, only three times does that verb *aphistēmi* mean a spiritual departure. For example, it is used of a spiritual departure in Luke 8:13 where it says, "Those on the rocky soil are those who, when they hear, receive the word with joy; and these have no firm root; they believe for a while, and in time of temptation fall away." "Fall away" is the English translation of *aphistēmi*, which refers to a spiritual departure. Similarly, First Timothy 4:1 says, "But the Spirit explicitly says that in latter times some will fall away from the faith, paying attention to deceitful spirits and doctrines of demons." Again, "fall away" or *aphistēmi* refers to a spiritual departure here. In addition, Hebrews 3:12 says, "Take care, brethren, that there not be in any one of you an evil, unbelieving heart that falls away from the living God." Again, "fall away" or *aphistēmi* refers to a spiritual departure apostasy.

However, the majority of times, or a full seventy-five percent of instances, where *aphistēmi*, is used in the Greek New Testament it does *not* refer to a spiritual departure, but rather to a physical departure. Thus, while this verb is used 15 times, only three times does it mean a spiritual departure. The remaining twelve times it clearly means a physical departure. For example, Luke 2:37 says, "and then as a widow to the age of eighty-four, she never left the temple." Here, *aphistēmi* is used to indicate that she never physically "left" the temple. Luke 4:13 also says, "When the devil had finished every temptation, he left Him until an opportune time." Here, *aphistēmi* or "left" is used to indicate the physical removal or departure of Satan from Jesus. Similarly, in Luke 13:27, Jesus says, "DEPART FROM ME ye workers of iniquity." Again, *aphistēmi* is used here in reference to their physical departure from Christ. Acts 5:38 similarly records Gamaliel saying, "So in the present case, I say to you, stay away from these men." In other words, *aphistēmi* is used to record Gamaliel's exhortation for the unbelieving Jews to physically remove themselves from the apostles and the early church. Acts 12:10 also says, regarding Peter, "...the angel departed from him." Again, *aphistēmi* is used to depict the angel's physical departure from Peter. Moreover, Acts 15:38 says, "But Paul kept insisting that they should not take him along with them who had deserted them...." Here, *aphistēmi* is used depicting Mark's earlier decision to leave the missionary team (Acts 13:13). What did Mark do on that first missionary journey? He did not spiritually depart. Rather, the primary meaning is that he physically departed from them. Acts 19:9 similarly says, "But when some were becoming hardened and disobedient, speaking evil of the Way before the people, he withdrew from them." Again, *aphistēmi* translated "withdrew" is used about a physical departure. Second Corinthians 12:8, concerning Paul's thorn in the flesh also says, "Concerning this

I implored the Lord three times that it might leave me." "Leave" is translated from the Greek verb *aphistēmi* and it again is speaking of Paul's desire for the Lord to remove this physical infirmity from him. What all these usages demonstrate is that both the noun *apostasia* and the verb *aphistēmi* can both be used to depict either spiritual departures or physical departures.

The Extended
Context Favors
a Physical
Departure
Interpretation
of *Apostasia*

S ince these words can be used in either sense, what rules should be used to determine which meaning to supply? While the three rules of real estate are "location, location, location," the three rules of Bible study interpretation are "context, context, context!" Context is king when determining the meanings of words. This is especially true since words frequently have multiple meanings.

Take the word "apple" as an example. Think how many meanings can be generated from the single word "apple." It can refer to a computer, a piece of fruit, the pupil of one's eye, and even New York City. So, when you see the word "apple" in a paragraph how do you know what meaning is in play? The context answers that question. If the word apple is found in a context dealing with computers, it would be invalid to substitute a fruit understanding into the word "apple." As another example, note how many different meanings there are for the word "run?"

> I **ran** out of ingredients for the salad, so I decided to make a quick **run** to the store. While at the store I left the car engine **running** while I made my purchase, thinking that I would be right out again. However, while I was in the store I **ran** into a good friend Edward who was **running** for county supervisor. This resulted in me having to endure a somewhat longwinded **rundown** on how his campaign was **running**. Finally fearing that the car would **run** out of gas I **ran** with great haste into the parking lot and returned home with the care surely **running** on fumes.[6]

Notice how the word "run" can radically change just within one paragraph. So how do we determine the meanings of words? They are entirely context driven. Therefore, we must be careful to

---

6 George A. Gunn, "Jesus and the Rapture: John 14," in *Evidence for the Rapture: A Biblical Case for Pretribulationism*, ed. John F. Hart (Chciago: Moody, 2015), 110.

determine the meaning of a word from its immediate context. Since, as has been demonstrated, the verb *aphistēmi* and the noun *apostasia* can both refer to either a physical departure or a spiritual departure let us now examine both the immediate and extended context of Second Thessalonians 2:3a to ascertain if a spiritual or physical departure is in view.

The extended context favors the meaning physical departure. What do I mean by "extended context"? I am referring to both books, First and Second Thessalonians, since both were written in close proximity to one another. Interestingly, in First Thessalonians every single chapter ends with a reference to the return of Jesus (1 Thess. 1:10; 2:19-20; 3:13; 4:13-18; 5:23-38). In fact, the most detailed treatment of the rapture that we have in the entire Bible is found at the end of the fourth chapter of First Thessalonians (4:13-18). Since the "context is king" in determining the meaning of the *apostasia* and the larger context of the Thessalonian letters pertain to the return of Christ, interpreters should be open to a physical departure understanding of the word. Thus, the larger context of these two books does not favor spiritual departure interpretation of the *apostasia*, but rather it favors the physical departure view.

7

The Immediate Context Favors a Physical Departure Interpretation of *Apostasia*

The immediate context also favors physical departure. What I mean by the "immediate context" is what is happening in the very same chapter and paragraph where the disputed term is located. Notice Second Thessalonians 2:1, which says, "Now we request you, brethren, with regard to the coming of our Lord Jesus Christ and our gathering together to Him." Here, Paul is speaking of our gathering to the Lord. In fact, this word translated "gathering" is *episynagōgē*, where we get the word synagogue. A synagogue is a Jewish gathering. Thus, verse one describes the context that will be dealt with in the rest of the chapter, which is the Lord coming to gather His church at the rapture.

Verses 6 and 7 continue with the same context when they say, "[6] And you know what restrains him now, so that in his time he will be revealed. [7] For the mystery of lawlessness is already at work; only he who now restrains will do so until he is taken out of the way." The Antichrist, Paul is saying, cannot come to power until the restrainer is first removed. Well then, who is the restrainer? Some say the restrainer is Rome. However, Rome is gone and the restraint is still present since the Antichrist has not yet come forward. Others say the restrainer is Satan, but why would the devil fight the Antichrist who is on the devil's side (2 Thess. 2:9)? Did not Jesus say a house divided against itself cannot stand (Matt. 12:25-26)? Still others contend that the restrainer is human government. However, as those living under tyrannical dictatorships will testify, human government many times does not restrain evil but rather contributes to it. Still others claim that the restrainer is Michael, the archangel. However, Jude 9 indicates that Michael does not typically openly contest or even argue with Satan.

Rather, he simply says the Lord rebuke you. [Jude 9, "But Michael the archangel, when he disputed with the devil and argued about the body of Moses, did not dare pronounce against him a railing judgment, but said, 'The Lord rebuke you!'"]

I believe that this restrainer is none other than the Holy Spirit, the third member of the Trinity. Several reasons lead me to this conclusion. *First*, the Holy Spirit is omnipotent deity (Acts 5:3-4). Only such omnipotent power could hold back the coming lawless one, who will be Satan's man of the hour and directly empowered by him (2 Thess. 2:9). *Second*, in the Greek text there is a switch in gender in the participle "restrainer" from neuter in verse 6 to masculine in verse 7. Such a switch in gender well describes the Holy Spirit because the Greek noun for spirit is *pneuma*, which is a neuter noun. However, Jesus in the Upper Room also referred to the Spirit through the masculine pronoun "He" (John 14:16). For example, in John 16:13 Jesus of the Holy Spirit said, "But when *He*, the Spirit of truth, comes, *He* will guide you into all the truth; for *He* will not speak on *His* own initiative, but whatever *He* hears, *He* will speak; and *He* will disclose to you what is to come" (italics added). *Third*, we know from other Scriptures that the Holy Spirit is very active in the world restraining evil the same way that the restrainer is depicted in Second Thessalonians 2:6-7. For example, the Holy Spirit was striving with man for one hundred and twenty years prior to the global Flood (Gen. 6:3). Moreover, it is the Holy Spirit that places men and women throughout the world under conviction in the present age to trust in Jesus Christ to receive personal salvation (John 16:7-11). Therefore, an understanding of the Holy Spirit as the restrainer fits very well with other verses describing the Spirit's activity of restraining evil in the world.

Thus, the restrainer that is now holding back the Antichrist is the omnipotent Holy Spirit. Where does the Holy Spirit live? He lives inside the child of God (Rom. 8:9) and He lives within us forever (John 14:16). The Holy Spirit permanently indwells all Christians. Thus, all Spirit indwelt Christians must be removed before the Antichrist can come to power. Paul, in verses six and seven is describing the physical departure of the church, which must transpire before the Antichrist can arrive on the scene.

In sum, the immediate context of the entire paragraph is the rapture of the church. Paul deals with this subject in both verse one as well as verses six and seven. If "context is king" and both the noun and the verb of *apostasia* can refer to a physical departure, it is only natural and logical to supply a physical departure understanding to this word in Second Thessalonians 2:3a. Such an interpretation finds ample support in both the extended and immediate context. Why would I read into this word *apostasia* a doctrinal departure when the context is very clear that he is dealing with subjects related to a physical departure?

8

Second Thessalonians 2:3a is Part of a Review Course

People sometimes ask, if the physical departure view is the correct interpretation of *apostasia* in Second Thessalonians 2:3a, then why does not this verse not simply say *harpazō* or "rapture"? The answer to this question relates to the fact that Paul employs numerous terms to describe the rapture in his writings. Examples include *ryhomai* (1 Thess. 1:10), *parousia* (2 Thess. 2:1), *episynagōgē* (2 Thess. 2:1), *apoka-lypsis* (1 Cor. 1:7), *epiphaneia* (Titus 2:13), and *harpazō* (1 Thess. 4:17). If Paul does use a variety of terms to depict the rapture, it should not be surprising to find him using another term like *apostasia* in Second Thess. 2:3a.

The answer to this question also relates to the fact that that Paul is giving a review type of course in Second Thessalonians 2. The Apostle Paul had already taught the Thessalonian believers about the rapture (1 Thess. 1:10; 4:13-18). Because Paul uses a variety of terms earlier in First and Second Thessalonians to describe the rapture (rescues, caught up, gathering, etc...), it's not surprising that he would use yet another term here. In fact, in Second Thessalonians 2:5, Paul unlocks the meaning of this entire passage. He says, "Do you not remember that while I was still with you I was telling you these things?" Unfortunately, there are many who say you should never teach new believers about Bible prophecy. Paul obviously did not embrace this view because he not only brought the Thessalonians to Christ, but he also began to teach them prophetic truths to such a degree that he asks later, "don't you remember that when I was with you I was telling you these things." What Paul is doing in Second Thessalonians 2 is he is reviewing ground that he has already covered. When you review prior ground you do not lay the fundamentals down all over again, do you? You do not use the identical vocabulary that you used previously. I am a teacher in a college and when I review for the test I do not re-teach all the material covered earlier in the semester. I use different words. What Paul is doing here is a review course, and that is why he does not use the identical language that he used to describe the rapture in First Thessalonians.

It is also worth noting that that the mere absence of the word *harpazō* should not, in and of itself, disqualify a passage, like Second Thessalonians 2:3a, from being a rapture passage since many commonly accepted rapture passages (John 14:1-3; 1 Thess. 1:10; 1 Cor. 15:50-58; Titus 2:13) also fail to employ the term *harpazō*. Moreover, many would also consider the catching up of the two witnesses during the Tribulation period as a type of a rapture (Rev. 11:12), even though the verb *harpazō* is not employed there either. In sum, understanding that Paul is using stylistically different words when reviewing material explains why the Apostle does not use terms previously used to describe the rapture such as "caught up" or *harpazō* (1 Thess. 4:17) and "rescues" or *ryhomai* (1 Thess. 1:10). Rather, Paul employs the stylistically different word *apostasia*, with the same meaning physical departure.

9

Early Bible Translations Favor the Physical Departure View

The earliest Bible translators all recognized the noun "apostasy" (2 Thess. 2:3a) as communicating physical departure. In fact, Jerome, going back to the fourth century, translated the New Testament from Greek into Latin in what is called the Latin Vulgate. It is called the Vulgate because Vulgate means common. Latin was the common language of the day. Jerome wanted the Bible readable in the common language of the day, which in the fourth century was Latin. From the word Vulgate, we get the word "vulgar," as in common, earthy speech. When Jerome translated Second Thessalonians 2:3a he used the Latin word *discessio*, which means departure.

Consequently, all the earliest English translations similarly translated the Greek noun *apostasia* in Second Thessalonians 2:3a as "departure" or "departing." The following early English Bible translations all translated *apostasia prōton* in Second Thessalonians 2:3a as "Departynge first": the Wycliffe Bible (1384), the Tyndale Bible (1526), the Coverdale Bible (1535), and the Cranmer Bible (1539). Similarly, the following early English Bible translations all translated *apostasia prōton* in Second Thessalonians 2:3a as "Departing first": the Breeches Bible (1576), the Beza Bible (1583), and the Geneva Bible (1608).[7] Thus, they all translated this noun, *apostasia*, as a physical departure in verse 3a.

How did a spiritual departure understanding of *apostasia* in Second Thessalonians 2:3a then enter the translation history of the English Bible versions? Thomas Ice offers the following explanation:

> Most scholars say that no one knows the reason for the translation shift. However, a plausible theory has been put forth by Martin Butalla in his Master of Theology thesis produced at Dallas Theology Seminary

---

7 House, 270.

in 1998. It appears that the Catholic translation into English from Jerome's Latin Vulgate known as the Rheims Bible (1576) was the first to break the translation trend. "*Apostasia* was revised from 'the departure' to 'the Protestant Revolt,'" explains Butalla. "Revolution is the terminology still in use today when Catholicism teaches the history of the Protestant Reformation. Under this guise, *apostasia* would refer to a departure of Protestants from the Catholic Church." The Catholic translators appear eager to engage in polemics against the Reformation by even allowing it to impact Bible translation.[8]

Thus, the shift from a physical to a spiritual understanding of *apostasia* in Second Thessalonians 2:3a in the Roman Catholic Rheims Bible English translation appears to have been theologically rather than exegetically motivated.

Furthermore, in 1611 the King James translators translated *apostasia* in Second Thessalonians 2:3a with the expression, "falling away." This is perhaps the second time that we begin to see a spiritual departure understanding of this verse enter an English translation. Why did the King James translators translate it as a spiritual departure when virtually everybody else, going back to Jerome, thought it was speaking of a physical departure? The answer most likely lies in the fact the KJV translation was created in the wake of the Protestant Reformation. Consequently, the translators wanted to apply the verse to the Roman Catholic Church, which represented a "falling away" from the truth. Thus, the translators of both the Rheims Bible and the KJV errantly embraced the theological interpretation "falling way" in lieu of the longstanding exegetical interpretation "departing" that had been faithfully handed down to them.

---

8   Thomas Ice, "The 'Departure' in 2 Thessalonians 2:3," online: www.pre-trib.org, accessed 7 May 2017, 2.

Most modern translations follow the pattern established by the King James Version. The New King James, NIV, RSV, ASV, the Jerusalem Bible, and the New American Standard Bible do not say "departure." Rather, they translate *apostasia* in Second Thessalonians 2:3a as a doctrinal or spiritual departure by using such language as "apostasy, falling away, revolt, rejection, or rebellion." Understanding this translation history helps explain why so many today have never heard of the physical departure view. The reason most today have never heard it before is because we are all today following modern English translations that follow the spiritual departing view found in the King James Version. However, the earliest English translations, and even the Latin translation of the Bible, going all the way back to the fourth century understood the *apostasia*, not as a spiritual falling away, but rather as a physical removal. For those living prior to the advent of the King James Version of 1611, most likely the more popular view that they would have been exposed to would have been the physical departure understanding of Second Thessalonians 2:3a rather than the spiritual departure interpretation.

10

The Physical Departure View is Held by Credible Scholars

Although it remains a minority position today, the physical departure view is still held by many credible Bible scholars. There are many luminaries that do hold to this view. Among them are the Greek scholar Kenneth Wuest as well as others such as John R. Rice, J. S. Mabie, E. Schuyler English, J. Dwight Pentecost, Paul Lee Tan, H. Wayne House, Stanley Ellison, Allen McRae, and Gordon Lewis. At the more popular level, both Tim LaHaye and Thomas Ice, hold to a physical departure interpretation as well.

Conclusion

What I am trying to get at is simply this: what Paul is saying in Second Thessalonians 2:3a is first, before the man of sin comes and the Tribulation period begins, there will be a physical departure of the church via the rapture. What Paul is saying to the beleaguered and bewildered Thessalonians who were deceived by forged letters allegedly having emanated from Paul indicating that the Day of the Lord had already begun, is that they could not possible be in the Tribulation period because they are still physically present on planet earth. In other words, the Thessalonians are not in the Tribulation period because the Tribulation period itself will not take place until there is first a physical removal of the church via the rapture.

Ten reasons cause me to hold to this position. No singular point in and of itself "seals the deal." However, when these ten points are considered cumulatively, a powerful case emerges that Paul is speaking of a physical departure through his use of the word *apostasia* in Second Thessalonians 2:3a. Since doctrinal departures would have been considered normative throughout the Church Age, how could that, in and of itself, be a definitive sign of the end? Also, the Thessalonian letters are very early letters, where Paul does not get into the subject of an end-time doctrinal or spiritual departure. Moreover, the definite article in front of the noun *apostasia* lends support to the physical departure view by conveying its instantaneous rather than gradual nature. In addition, because both the noun and the verb emanating from the same root can be used very clearly to refer to physical departures, the extended context and the immediate context must be consulted to define the meaning of *apostasia* in Second Thessalonians 2:3a. Also, both the extended context and the immediate context favor the physical departure rendering of *apostasia*. Moreover, Paul does not use the same word "rapture" that he used earlier since 2 Thessalonians 2 is merely a review session. Also, early Bible translations favor the physical departure view. Finally, the physical departure view is held by credible scholars.

If what I have said is true, then it is time to stop debating the timing of the rapture. The debate is settled. The rapture of the church will take place "first" before the Tribulation period begins. We can develop certainty in the return of Jesus Christ to take us out of the world physically before the events of the Tribulation period transpire. Titus 2:13 is indeed our firm blessed hope, which says, "looking for the blessed hope and the appearing of the glory of our great God and Savior, Christ Jesus."

Select Bibliography

Barton, David. *Original Intent: The Courts, the Constitution, & Religion.* 3d ed. Aledo, TX: Wall Builder Press, 2000.

English, E. Schuyler. *Re-Thinking the Rapture: An Examination of What the Scriptures Teach as to the Time of the Translation of the Church in Relation to the Tribulation.* Neptune, NJ: Loizeaux Brothers, 1954.

Gunn, George A. "Jesus and the Rapture: John 14." In *Evidence for the Rapture: A Biblical Case for Pretribulationism*, edited by John F. Hart, 99-121. Chciago: Moody, 2015.

House, H. Wayne. "Apostasia in 2 Thessalonians 2:3: Apostasy of Rapture?" In *When the Trumpet Sounds: Today's Foremost Authorities Speak out on End Time Controversies*, edited by Thomas Ice and Timothy Demy, 262-96. Eugene, OR: Harvest House, 1995.

Lampe, G. W. H. *A Patristic Greek Lexicon.* Oxford: Clarnedon Press, 1961.

Woods, Andy. "2 Thessalonians 2:3a: Apostasy of Rapture?" *The Prophecy Watcher* May 2017, 14-17, 34-35.

Dispensational Publishing House is striving to become the go-to source for Bible-based materials from the dispensational perspective.

Our goal is to provide high-quality doctrinal and worldview resources that make dispensational theology accessible to people at all levels of understanding.

Visit our blog regularly to read informative articles from both known and new writers.

And please let us know how we can better serve you.

Dispensational Publishing House, Inc.
PO Box 3181
Taos, NM 87571

Call us toll free 844-321-4202

CPSIA information can be obtained
at www.ICGtesting.com
Printed in the USA
LVHW021933190720
661002LV00015B/562